Contents

4	Introduction
6	**Tasty Treats for Little Treasures**
8	Linda's Liver Sausage Biscuits
10	Herby Fish Hearts
12	Dixie's Cheese Crunchies
14	Buttermilk Snacks
16	Pauline's Cheese Dreams
18	Crunchy Pumpkin Crescents
22	**Healthy Bites**
24	Bonnie's Banana Biscuits
26	Sammy's Anchovy Purses
28	Apple and Carrot Dumplings
30	Tofu Strips à la Tiffany
32	Benji's Rice Crackers
34	Dexter's Spinach Biscuits
36	**Hearty Nibbles**
38	Pippa's Tripe Biscuits
40	Crunchy Sesame Bites
42	Reward Biscuits
46	Samantha's Scones
48	Bobby's Brownies
50	Muesli Rolls
52	**Chewy Fun for Great Friends**
54	Scamp's Minced Beef Biscuits
56	Willy's Wheat Crescents
58	Gina's Polenta Biscuits with Liver Sausage
60	Crispy Bacon Rolls
62	Billy's Crunchy Bones
64	Bella's Almond Cantuccini
66	**Extra Treats for Greedy Gourmets**
68	Christmas Sausage Biscuits
70	Gus's Poultry Nibbles
72	Mimi's Muesli Muffins
74	Susie's Juicy Christmas Cakes
76	Toby's Tuna Triangles
78	Freda's Fine Birthday Fish Tarts
80	Index

Introduction

Baking is love – these words, from an advertising slogan of the last century, may seem a bit exaggerated to many readers when applied to the well-being of our four-legged friends. However, baking always has something to do with warmth, closeness and affection.

When the scent of Pauline's cheese dreams or Linda's liver sausage biscuits emanates from my kitchen and fills the house, my four-legged housemate Dexter becomes very lively and will not leave his observation post just outside the kitchen until he gets to try a few tasters – still warm – of my new biscuit creations. And I am sure he is grateful when I bake him a special treat now and then. So we both feel happy.

Of course, you can look at the baking of dog treats in a purely pragmatic manner. The home-made biscuits are usually cheaper than bought ones, and they contain no preservatives or flavour enhancers. For children, baking biscuits is an enjoyable way to pass the time, and adults can escape a little from their daily routine by kneading and shaping the dough.

The same applies to biscuits and cakes as to all extra treats: too much is not good for your dog. It doesn't matter how healthy the ingredients are: they cannot and should not replace your dog's normal diet, only supplement it. If you care for your dog's health, then feed it biscuits only in carefully measured quantities – and ignore that pleading, begging look in your dog's eyes.

Some things should never be included in dog treats: chemical additives, spicy seasoning, white sugar, chocolate and cocoa should never be put in the dog bowl or into your baked dog treats. Apart from that, your creativity in baking need know few bounds. As our home-made biscuits don't contain preservatives, they will not keep forever. We let a lot of the biscuits dry out in the oven after baking, to let them harden. This means that the dogs have more fun chewing them and also, when biting, clean their teeth. For older dogs, take the biscuits out of the oven straight away and let them cool on a rack.

Some tasty treats from the oven are intended to be eaten quickly. When we bake these recipes, we distribute them generously to all dogs that we like – even if my own dog Dexter is not exactly in favour of this rule.

Baking for your dog can make you and your dog happy and is easy, even for beginners. We had lots of fun in our kitchen and would like to take this opportunity to thank all dogs whose lip-smacking agreement or simple refusal of food has contributed to the quality of the dog treats in this book. A very special thank you is owed to my sister Monika and niece Julia. Not only did they bake all the biscuits in many different variations, but also they tirelessly tested and further refined their creations in a circle of dog-loving friends.

Ingeborg Pils

DOGGIE BISCUITS

HEALTHY HOMEMADE TREATS – SEASONED WITH AFFECTION

Ingeborg Pils

PaRragon

Bath · New York · Singapore · Hong Kong · Cologne · Delhi · Melbourne

All recipes in this book have been carefully put together with advice from veterinary surgeons and tried out on different dogs. However, it is not impossible that in individual cases some meals may have negative consequences.

The publishers and the author can accept no liability for such consequences.

Not everything that human beings like to consume is good for dogs. Indisputably harmful are alcohol, cocoa, garlic, raisins, the onion family, chocolate with a high proportion of cocoa butter, raw pork and hot spicy dishes. A few studies and Internet pages now classify further foodstuffs as poorly tolerated by dogs. Other sources – the veterinary surgeons we consulted among them – disagree with these opinions.

If you are in any way uncertain how well your dog will tolerate any of the ingredients, please consult your vet.

This edition published in 2010
Copyright © Parragon Books Ltd 2009
Parragon Publishing
Queen Street House,
4 Queen Street, Bath BA1 1HE, UK

Production: ditter.projektagentur GmbH
Project coordination: Michael Ditter
Food photography: Jo Kirchherr; **Food styling:** Rafael Pranschke;
Illustrations: Kyra Stempell; **Design:** Sabine Vonderstein;
Lithography: Klausner Medien Service GmbH

UK edition produced by Cambridge Publishing Management Ltd
Translator: Sue James

The publisher wishes to express particular thanks to Dr. Burton Miller, renown holistic doctor of veterinary medicine, for his careful advice on the recipes included in this book. Based in Huntington, NY, Dr. Miller is the founder of the Animal Wellness Center (www.animalwellness.net).

ISBN: 978-1-4075-5236-1

Printed in China

TASTY TREATS FOR LITTLE TREASURES

LINDA'S LIVER SAUSAGE BISCUITS

Makes about 40 biscuits

100 g (3½ oz) coarse rolled oats
100 g (3½ oz) fine rolled oats
150 g (5 oz) cottage cheese
100 g (3½ oz) liver sausage
6 tablespoons corn oil
1 egg

Mix all the ingredients to make a dough. It should not be too firm. If required, add a little extra water or flour.

Line a baking tray with baking parchment. Shape the dough into little balls, place them on the baking paper and flatten them. Place them in the cold oven, set it to 180°C (350°F) (with fan) and bake for 30 minutes.

Let the liver sausage biscuits cool on a wire rack. Keep them in a biscuit tin. If your dog permits, the liver sausage biscuits will keep for about 3 weeks.

Herby Fish Hearts

Makes about 35 hearts

100 g (3½ oz) cooked fish, without bones
3 tablespoons finely chopped fresh herbs
2 tablespoons extra virgin olive oil
1 egg
200 g (7 oz) spelt flour
100 g (3½ oz) ground hazelnuts

Purée the fish and the herbs in a food processor. Put the purée in a bowl, then stir in the olive oil and the egg. Add the flour and nuts, then mix all the ingredients to make a smooth dough. Shape the dough into a ball, wrap it in cling film and let it rest for 30 minutes.

Preheat the oven to 180°C (350°F). Line a baking tray with baking parchment.

On a floured surface, roll out the dough until about 8 mm (¼ inch) thick. With a biscuit cutter, cut out little heart shapes. Place these on the baking tray and bake in the oven for 30 minutes.

Let the fish hearts cool on a wire rack. Store in a biscuit tin; they will keep for about 2 weeks.

DIXIE'S CHEESE CRUNCHIES

Makes about 30 crunchies

100 g (3½ oz) chopped almonds
100 g (3½ oz) roughly chopped hazelnuts
150 g (5 oz) grated Emmental cheese
4 eggs
550 g (1 lb 3 oz) buckwheat flour
1 tablespoon honey
water and flour as required

Toast the almonds and hazelnuts in a non-stick pan, without oil or fat, until a light brown. Remove from the heat and let them cool.

Knead the nuts in with the remaining ingredients to form a smooth dough.
If required, add a little more water or flour, depending on whether the dough is too dry or too moist.

Preheat the oven to 160°C (320°F). Line a baking sheet with baking parchment.

On a floured surface, roll out the dough to about 1 cm (½ inch) thick. Using a pastry wheel, cut into rectangles about 2 cm x 5 cm (¾ inch x 2 inches) in size.

Place the biscuits on the baking sheet. Bake for 1 hour. Turn off the heat and let the biscuits dry for another hour in the oven. Store in a paper or linen bag; they will keep for about 4 weeks.

BUTTERMILK SNACKS

Makes about 35 snacks

250 g (9 oz) chicken livers
1 tablespoon sunflower oil
100 ml (3 fl oz) buttermilk
250 g (9 oz) wholegrain flour

Chop the liver very finely (use a food processor or meat grinder), then stir in the sunflower oil and buttermilk. Add the flour and knead all the ingredients together to make a smooth dough. Cover the dough and let it rest in the fridge for 30 minutes.

Line a baking sheet with baking parchment.

On a floured surface, roll out the dough to about 1 cm (½ inch) thick. Use biscuit cutters – any shape you like – to cut out shapes. Place the biscuits on the baking sheet.

Bake the snacks at 180°C (350°F) (with fan) for 30 minutes. Turn off the oven and let the biscuits dry in the oven for another hour. Store in a biscuit tin. The snacks will keep for about 2 weeks.

PAULINE'S CHEESE DREAMS

Makes about 40 cheese dreams

125 g (4½ oz) cottage cheese
75 g (2½ oz) grated Parmesan cheese
300 g (11 oz) all-purpose flour
2 tablespoons vegetable oil
100 g (3½ oz) finely chopped hazelnuts

Preheat the oven to 200°C (400°F). Line a baking sheet with baking parchment.

Put all the ingredients into a bowl and mix well using the dough hooks on a hand-held mixer. Use 2 teaspoons to shape little portions of the dough and place the shapes on the baking sheet.

Bake the biscuits for 30 minutes. Turn off the oven and let the biscuits dry for another 2 hours in the oven. Store in a paper or linen bag. The cheese dreams will keep for about 4 weeks.

CRUNCHY PUMPKIN CRESCENTS

Makes about 35 crescents

3 potatoes, boiled unpeeled
150 g (5 oz) cooked pumpkin flesh
100 g (3½ oz) veal or pork sausage meat
100 g (3½ oz) wholewheat flour
3 tablespoons vegetable oil
1 egg
50 g (2 oz) pumpkin seeds

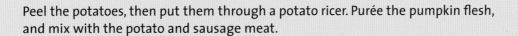

Peel the potatoes, then put them through a potato ricer. Purée the pumpkin flesh, and mix with the potato and sausage meat.

Add flour, oil and the egg, then knead all the ingredients to make a smooth dough. Cover and let rest for 30 minutes.

Preheat the oven to 180°C (350°F). Line a baking sheet with baking parchment.

On a floured surface, roll out the dough until about 1 cm (½ inch) thick and use a biscuit cutter to make crescent shapes. Place the biscuits on the baking sheet and decorate with pumpkin seeds.

Bake the pumpkin crescents for 25 minutes. Turn off the heat and let the biscuits dry in the oven for another 2 hours.

'My dog is dearest to my heart,
My heart,
Man says it is a sin,
My dog is true in the tempest of life,
And Man not even in the wind.'

St Francis of Assisi

HEALTHY
BITES

Bonnie's Banana Biscuits

Makes about 30 biscuits

2 carrots
1 banana
200 g (7 oz) all-purpose flour
100 g (3½ oz) fine rolled oats
50 ml (1½ fl oz) sunflower oil
water as required

Grate the carrots finely and mash the banana with a fork. Mix to make a dough with the flour, rolled oats and oil. If necessary, add a little water.

Preheat the oven to 180°C (350°F). Line a baking sheet with baking parchment.

On a floured surface, roll out the dough to about 1 cm (½ inch) thick and cut squares about 4 cm (1½ inches) in size. Place these on the sheet and bake for 25 minutes. Turn off the heat and let them cool overnight in the oven. Store in a paper or linen bag. The biscuits will keep for about 3 weeks.

SAMMY'S ANCHOVY PURSES

Makes about 15 purses

150 g (5 oz) quark
3 tablespoons milk
2 tablespoons fish oil
4 tablespoons safflower oil
300 g (11 oz) wholewheat flour
15 anchovy fillets
100 g (3½ oz) cottage cheese
1 egg white

Stir the quark into the milk, fish oil and safflower oil. Gradually stir in half the flour into the cheese mixture, then knead in the rest. Cover the dough and let it rest for 30 minutes.

Preheat the oven to 200°C (400°F). Line a baking sheet with baking parchment.

On a floured surface, roll out the dough and cut out 30 circles with a biscuit cutter. Rinse the anchovy fillets in cold water, then place them on half the dough circles and cover each with some of the cottage cheese. Paint the edges of the circles with the egg white. Cover with the remaining circles and press the edges firmly together.

Place the dough purses on the baking sheet and bake for 25 minutes. Turn off the heat and let them dry in the oven. Store in a biscuit tin.

The purses will keep for about 5 days.

APPLE AND CARROT DUMPLINGS

Makes about 40 dumplings

1 apple
1 carrot
150 g (5 oz) spelt flour
150 g (5 oz) coarse rolled oats
2 eggs
3 tablespoons molasses
water and flour as required

Finely grate the apple and carrot, then mix with the other ingredients to make an easily shaped dough. If necessary, add a little extra water or flour.

Preheat the oven to 180°C (350°F). Line a baking sheet with baking parchment.

Use 2 teaspoons to shape the mixture into little dumplings and place the dumplings on the baking sheet. Bake for 30 minutes, then turn off the heat and let the dumplings dry in the oven. Store in a paper or linen bag. The dumplings will keep for about 3 weeks.

TOFU STRIPS À LA TIFFANY

Makes about 35 strips

200 g (7 oz) tofu
3 carrots
3 tablespoons linseed oil
2 eggs
250 g (9 oz) wholewheat flour
1 tablespoon chopped rosemary

Crumble the tofu and grate the carrots. Purée in a blender with the linseed oil.
Knead the eggs and flour into the purée. Knead the chopped rosemary into
the dough.

Preheat the oven to 180°C (350°F). Line a baking sheet with baking parchment.

On a floured surface, roll out the dough to about 5 mm (¼ inch) thick and use
a pastry wheel to cut strips about 2 cm x 7 cm (¾ inch x 2¾ inches). Place on
the baking sheet and bake for 30 minutes. Turn the strips halfway through the
baking time.

Let the tofu strips cool on a wire rack. Store in a biscuit tin. The strips will keep for
about 2 weeks.

BENJI'S RICE CRACKERS

Makes about 35 crackers

3 small courgettes
300 g (11 oz) cooked short-grain rice
200 g (7 oz) quark
1 egg
200 g (7 oz) wholewheat flour

Finely grate the courgettes. Mix them with the rice, quark and egg, then gradually work in the flour.

Preheat the oven to 200°C (400°F). Line a baking tray with baking parchment.

On a floured surface, roll out the dough to about 2 cm (¾ inch) thick and cut it into 4 cm (1½ inch) squares. Place the squares on the baking sheet and bake for 40 minutes. Then turn off the heat and let the crackers dry out overnight in the oven. Store in a paper or linen bag. The crackers will keep for about 2 weeks.

DEXTER'S SPINACH BISCUITS

Makes about 40 biscuits

125 g (4½ oz) frozen spinach
2 tablespoons grated Parmesan cheese
100 g (3½ oz) all-purpose flour
100 g (3½ oz) fine rolled oats
water and flour as required

Cook the spinach in a little water, then drain it thoroughly and purée in a blender. Mix the spinach purée with the remaining ingredients to make an easily shaped dough. If necessary, add a little water or flour.

Preheat the oven to 180°C (350°F). Line a baking sheet with baking parchment.

Shape little portions of the dough with a spoon and place them on the baking sheet. Bake in the oven for about 30 minutes.

Let the spinach biscuits cool on a wire tray and store in a biscuit tin. The biscuits will keep for about 2 weeks.

HEARTY
NIBBLES

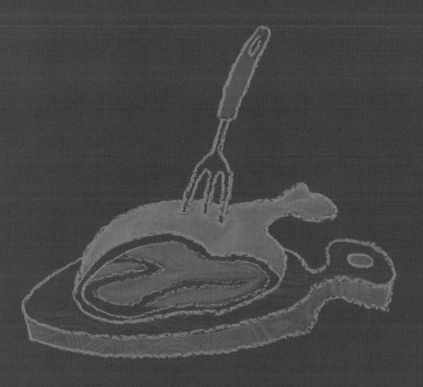

PIPPA'S TRIPE BISCUITS

Makes about 40 biscuits

200 ml (6 fl oz) hot water
200 g (7 oz) polenta
100 g (3½ oz) cornflour
50 g (2 oz) tripe, finely chopped
1 egg

Pour the hot water over the polenta, stir and let cool. Then knead in the other ingredients.

Preheat the oven to 180°C (350°F). Line a baking sheet with baking paper.

On a floured surface, roll out the dough to about 1 cm (½ inch) thick and cut it into triangles. Place these on the baking sheet and bake for 25 minutes. Turn off the heat and let the biscuits dry for a few hours in the oven. Store in a screw-topped glass jar or in a biscuit tin. The biscuits will keep for about 4 weeks.

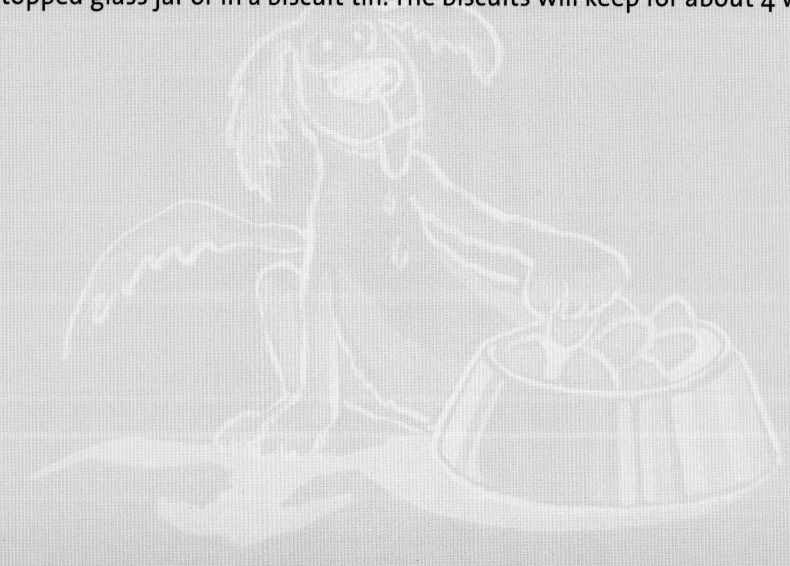

CRUNCHY SESAME BITES

Makes about 30 bites

250 g (9 oz) spelt flour
100 g (3½ oz) grated Emmental cheese
80 g (3 oz) low-fat quark
2 eggs
30 g (1 oz) sesame seeds

Knead all the ingredients, except for the sesame seeds, together to form an easily shaped dough. Make small, thumb-sized rolls from the dough and press one side into the sesame seeds.

Preheat the oven to 180°C (350°F). Line a baking sheet with baking parchment.

Place the sesame bites on the baking sheet and bake for 30 minutes. Turn off the heat and leave the bites to dry overnight in the oven. Store in a paper or linen bag. The sesame bites will keep for about 3 weeks.

REWARD BISCUITS

Makes about 35 biscuits

100 g (3½ oz) wholewheat flour
100 g (3½ oz) coarse rolled oats
2 tablespoons oat bran
2 eggs
75 g (2½ oz) grated Parmesan cheese
75 g (2½ oz) finely diced ham
100 ml (3 fl oz) water

Mix all the ingredients with the water to make a smooth dough. Cover and let the dough rest for about 30 minutes.

Preheat the oven to 180°C (350°F). Line a baking sheet with baking parchment.

On a floured surface, roll out the dough to about 1 cm (½ inch) thick and cut into 3 cm x 5 cm (1¼ x 2 inch) rectangles. Place these on the baking sheet and bake for 25 minutes. Turn off the heat and let the biscuits harden in the oven for another 2 hours. Store in a paper or linen bag. The biscuits will keep for about 4 weeks.

'As long as human beings think that animals do not feel, animals have to feel that human beings cannot think.'

Arthur Schopenhauer

SAMANTHA'S SCONES

Makes about 12 scones

150 g (5 oz) all-purpose flour
1 egg
100 g (3½ oz) wholegrain flour
3 teaspoons baking powder
1 teaspoon chopped seaweed
1 tablespoon brewer's yeast
150 ml (5 fl oz) milk
50 g (2 oz) butter

Knead all the ingredients to make a smooth dough. Let the dough rest for 10 minutes. Preheat the oven to 200°C (400°F). Line a baking sheet with baking parchment.

On a floured surface, roll out the dough to about 2 cm (¾ inch) thick and cut out round biscuit shapes with a glass about 5 cm (2 inches) in diameter. Place the shapes on the baking tray and bake for 10 minutes.

Let the scones cool on a wire tray.

BOBBY'S BROWNIES

Makes about 30 brownies

200 g (7 oz) wholewheat flour
200 g (7 oz) spelt flour
100 g (3½ oz) chopped walnuts
2 eggs
2 tablespoons sunflower oil
2 tablespoons molasses
½ sachet of dried yeast
water and flour as required

In a food processor, mix all the ingredients to form a firm dough. If necessary, add a little extra flour or water. Shape the dough into a ball and let it rise in a warm spot for 1 hour.

Preheat the oven to 160°C (320°F). Line a shallow rectangular baking pan with baking parchment.

Spread the dough over the baking pan until about 4 cm (1½ inches) thick. Bake for 35 minutes, then let it cool for 1 hour, still in the baking pan.

Turn out the baked cake, with the baking parchment, onto a board. Remove the baking parchment and cut the cake into dog bite-sized pieces. Store in a paper or linen bag. The brownies will keep for about 4 weeks.

MUESLI ROLLS

Makes about 30 rolls

1 apple
1 pear
100 g (3½ oz) all-purpose flour
100 g (3½ oz) coarse rolled oats
75 g (2½ oz) chopped hazelnuts
1 tablespoon honey
100 g (3½ oz) cottage cheese
50 g (2 oz) flax seeds

Roughly grate the apple and pear. Mix with the other ingredients, except for the flax seeds. With a tablespoon, take little portions of the dough and make roll shapes.

Preheat the oven to 180°C (350°F). Line a baking sheet with baking parchment.

Roll the muesli rolls in the flax seeds, place them on the baking tray and flatten them. Bake for 30 minutes, then turn off the heat and let the rolls cool in the oven. Store in a paper or linen bag. The muesli rolls will keep for about 3 weeks.

CHEWY FUN
FOR
GREAT FRIENDS

Scamp's Minced Beef Biscuits

Makes about 20 biscuits

300 g (11 oz) wholewheat flour
2 tablespoons mixed dried herbs
2 tablespoons safflower oil
1 egg
75 g (2½ oz) sunflower seeds
150 ml (5 fl oz) water
200 g (7 oz) minced beef

Preheat the oven to 200°C (400°F). Line a baking sheet with baking parchment.

Mix all the ingredients except for the sunflower seeds with 150 ml (5 fl oz) water to make a dough. On a floured surface, roll out the pastry to about 2 cm (¾ inch) thick and cut it into 3 cm x 6 cm (1¼ x 2¼ inch) rectangles. Press one side into the sunflower seeds and place with the other side downwards onto the baking sheet.

Bake the biscuits for 40 minutes. Turn off the heat and let the biscuits harden overnight in the oven. Store in a biscuit tin. The biscuits will keep for about 2 weeks.

WILLY'S WHEAT CRESCENTS

Makes about 35 crescents

100 g (3½ oz) all-purpose flour
150 g (5 oz) wholewheat flour
100 g (3½ oz) wheatgerm
3 tablespoons sunflower oil
250 ml (8½ fl oz) unsalted vegetable stock
75 g (2½ oz) cracked bulgur wheat

Mix both types of flour, the wheat germ and the oil,
pour on the stock and mix to make a smooth dough.
Cover the dough and let it rest for 20 minutes.

Preheat the oven to 200°C (400°F). Line a baking sheet with baking parchment.

Form the dough into a long roll and cut into slices. Shape the slices into balls,
then roll them into sausage shapes and wind them around your forefinger
to form crescents. Roll them in the bulgur wheat and place them on the
baking sheet.

Bake for 30 minutes. Turn off the heat and let the crescents dry out in the oven
for another 2 hours. Store in a paper or linen bag. The crescents will keep for about
4 weeks.

GINA'S POLENTA BISCUITS WITH LIVER SAUSAGE

Makes about 40 biscuits

250 ml (8½ fl oz) water
150 g (5 oz) polenta
150 g (5 oz) cornflour
100 g (3½ oz) canned sweetcorn, drained
100 g (3½ oz) coarse liver sausage
50 g (2 oz) lard
1 egg

Bring the water to the boil. Mix the polenta with the water and let it soak.
When the polenta has cooled, mix with the remaining ingredients.

Preheat the oven to 180°C (350°F). Line a baking sheet with baking parchment.

On a floured surface, roll out the dough to about 2 cm (¾ inch) thick and cut
out circles with a biscuit cutter. Place these on the baking sheet and bake for
30 minutes. Turn off the heat and let the biscuits harden overnight in the oven.
Store in a screw-topped glass jar or a biscuit tin. The biscuits will keep for about
2 weeks.

CRISPY BACON ROLLS

Makes about 30 rolls

150 g (5 oz) wholewheat flour
150 g (5 oz) wholegrain rye flour
75 g (2½ oz) wheat grains
75 g (2½ oz) bacon cubes
1 tablespoon brewer's yeast
3 tablespoons safflower oil
250 ml (8½ fl oz) unsalted meat stock
75 g (2½ oz) cracked bulgur wheat

Thoroughly mix all the ingredients except for the bulgur wheat. Cover the dough and let it rest for 30 minutes.

Preheat the oven to 180°C (350°F). Line a baking sheet with baking parchment.

Take portions of the dough with a large spoon and shape into rolls. Roll them in the bulgur wheat. Place them on the baking sheet and bake for 45 minutes. Turn off the heat and let them dry in the oven until they are quite hard. Store in a paper or linen bag. The rolls will keep for about 3 weeks.

BILLY'S CRUNCHY BONES

Makes about 6 'bones'

1 bunch watercress
400 g (14 oz) wholewheat flour
100 g (3½ oz) coarse rolled oats
50 g (2 oz) wheatgerm
50 g (2 oz) sunflower seeds
50 g (2 oz) lard
250 ml (8½ fl oz) unsalted meat stock

Finely chop the watercress. Knead it in with the other ingredients to form a dough. Roll out the dough to a thickness of about 2 cm (¾ inch) and cut out 6 bone-shaped pieces with a sharp knife.

Preheat the oven to 180°C (350°F). Line a baking sheet with baking parchment.

Place the 'bones' on the baking tray and bake for 45 minutes. Turn off the heat and let the bone shapes dry in the oven overnight. Store in a paper or linen bag. The 'bones' will keep for about 2 weeks.

BELLA'S ALMOND CANTUCCINI

Makes about 40 cantuccini

200 g (7 oz) cornflour
100 g (3½ oz) chopped almonds
1 egg
1 tablespoon honey
1 tablespoon extra virgin olive oil
1 tablespoon molasses
water as required

Knead all the ingredients together to make a smooth dough, adding a little water
if required. Shape the dough into a roll, wrap it in cling film and let it rest for
1 hour in the fridge.

Preheat the oven to 180°C (350°F). Line a baking sheet with baking parchment.

Cut the roll of dough into slices about 1 cm (½ inch) thick and place these on the
baking sheet. Bake for about 30 minutes in the preheated oven, then turn off
the heat and let the cantuccini dry in the oven. Store in a paper or linen bag. The
cantuccini will keep for about 4 weeks.

EXTRA TREATS FOR GREEDY GOURMETS

CHRISTMAS SAUSAGE BISCUITS

Makes about 30 biscuits

250 g (9 oz) wholegrain rye flour
100 g (3½ oz) rolled oats
30 g (1 oz) lard
100 g (3½ oz) sausage meat
200 ml (6 fl oz) water

Mix the ingredients with the water and knead them to make a firm dough. Shape the dough into a ball, wrap it in cling film and let it rest in the fridge for 30 minutes.

Preheat the oven to 160°C (320°F). Line a baking sheet with baking parchment.

On a floured surface, roll out the dough to a thickness of about 1 cm (½ inch) and use a biscuit cutter to cut out biscuit shapes. Place these on the baking sheet and bake for 40 minutes. Turn off the heat and let the biscuits dry in the oven. Store in a biscuit tin. The biscuits will keep for about 2 weeks.

Gus's Poultry Nibbles

Makes about 30 nibbles

400 g (14 oz) chicken or turkey breast

Cut the meat into thin strips with a sharp knife. Preheat the oven to 150°C (300°F).

Line a baking sheet with baking parchment and place the strips of meat on it side by side. Roast in the oven for 30–40 minutes.

Reduce the oven temperature to 100°C (210°F) and wedge a wooden spoon in the oven door to let the moisture escape. Let the strips of meat dry out for another 2 hours in the oven. Remove the baking sheet and let the strips of meat finish drying out overnight at room temperature. Keep in the fridge. The strips will keep for about 4 days.

MIMI'S MUESLI MUFFINS

Makes 24 muffins

250 g (9 oz) rolled oats
100 g (3½ oz) wholewheat flour
125 g (4½ oz) cracked bulgur wheat
2 tablespoons oat germ
3 teaspoons baking powder
3 tablespoons maple syrup
1 egg
2 bananas
100 g (3½ oz) blueberries
100 ml (3 fl oz) water

And also:
2 mini-muffin sheets, each for 12 muffins

Knead all the ingredients (except for the fruit) together to make a dough. Mash the bananas with a fork and mix into the dough. Finally, mix in the blueberries.

Preheat the oven to 180°C (350°F).

Distribute the dough among the moulds in the mini-muffin sheet and bake for 30 minutes. Tip out the muffins onto a wire rack and let them cool. Store in a biscuit tin. The muffins will keep for about 4 days.

SUSIE'S JUICY CHRISTMAS CAKES

Makes 6 cakes

250 g (9 oz) dried fruit (no raisins)
A little lukewarm water
250 g (9 oz) hazelnuts
100 g (3½ oz) unsweetened dried coconut flakes
2 tablespoons molasses
2 eggs
125 g (4½ oz) wholewheat flour
2 tablespoons breadcrumbs

Soak the dried fruit for 30 minutes in the water.
Then pour into a sieve, drain well and chop coarsely.
Mix the dried fruit with the other ingredients to make
a dough, and let it rest for 30 minutes.

Preheat the oven to 180°C (350°F).

Divide the dough into 6 portions. Shape into round, flat little cakes and place these on
a baking sheet. Bake for 40 minutes, then tip the cakes onto a wire rack for cooling.
Store in a biscuit tin. The cakes will keep for about 2 weeks.

TOBY'S TUNA TRIANGLES

Makes about 40 triangles

1 can tuna fish in natural juice
4 tablespoons extra virgin olive oil
1 egg
1 teaspoon dried thyme
1 teaspoon dried oregano
250 g (9 oz) cornflour
150 g (5 oz) rolled oats
50 g (2 oz) flour

Drain the tuna in a sieve, then purée it with the oil and the egg in a blender.
Mix the purée with the other ingredients to make a dough.

Preheat the oven to 180°C (350°F). Line a baking sheet with baking parchment.

Roll out the dough to about 1 cm (½ inch) thick and cut it into triangles. Place the
biscuits on the baking sheet and bake for 25 minutes. Store in a biscuit tin. The triangles
will keep for about 2 weeks.

FREDA'S FINE BIRTHDAY FISH TARTS

Makes 6 tarts

300 g (11 oz) pearl barley
water
200 g (7 oz) cooked fillet of fish
1 egg
2 tablespoons corn starch
2 tablespoons finely chopped mixed herbs

And also:
6 non-stick small tart moulds 12 cm (5 inches)
in diameter

Soak the pearl barley for 35 minutes in the water, then drain
well in a sieve.

Preheat the oven to 180°C (350°F).

Break up the fish fillet into small pieces with a fork and mix it with the pearl barley,
egg, corn starch and herbs. Divide the dough into 6 portions, put these into the tart
moulds and bake for 40 minutes. Then turn off the heat and let the tarts cool in their
moulds in the oven. Store in a biscuit tin. The tarts will keep for about 3 days.

Vegetarian

Apple and Carrot Dumplings	28
Bella's Almond Cantuccini	64
Benji's Rice Crackers	32
Bobby's Brownies	48
Bonnie's Banana Biscuits	24
Crunchy Sesame Bites	40
Dexter's Spinach Biscuits	34
Dixie's Cheese Crunchies	12
Mimi's Muesli Muffins	72
Muesli Rolls	50
Pauline's Cheese Dreams	16
Reward Biscuits	42
Samantha's Scones	46
Susie's Juicy Christmas Cakes	74
Tofu Strips à la Tiffany	30
Willy's Wheat Crescents	56

With Fish

Freda's Fine Birthday Fish Tarts	78
Herby Fish Hearts	10
Sammy's Anchovy Purses	26
Toby's Tuna Triangles	76

With Meat or Sausage Meat

Billy's Crunchy Bones	62
Buttermilk Snacks	14
Christmas Sausage Biscuits	68
Crispy Bacon Rolls	60
Crunchy Pumpkin Crescents	18
Gina's Polenta Biscuits with Liver Sausage	58
Gus's Poultry Nibbles	70
Linda's Liver Sausage Biscuits	8
Pippa's Tripe Biscuits	38
Scamp's Minced Beef Biscuits	54

Picture credits
Corbis: 1 William Geddes/Beateworks, 6 Flint, 21 DLILLC,
22 Ursula Klawitter/zefa, 36 Ursula Klawitter/zefa,
46 BreBa/bilderlounge, 52 Grove Pashly/Brand X,
66 Ursula Klawitter/zefa